Living The Easter Faith

Sermons For The Easter Season

Donald William Dotterer

CSS Publishing Company, Inc.
Lima, Ohio

Copyright © 1994 by
The CSS Publishing Company, Inc.
Lima, Ohio

Library of Congress Cataloging-in-Publication Data

Dotterer, Donald William.
    Living the Easter faith : sermons for the Easter season / by Donald W. Dotterer.
      p.   cm.
    Includes bibliographical references.
    ISBN 1-55673-522-7
    1. Easter—Sermons. 2. Eastertide—Sermons. 3. Sermons, American. I. Title.
BV4259.D67   1994
252'.63—dc20
                                   93-30842
                                      CIP

ISBN 1-55673-522-7

For my sons Steven and Andrew, who share the joy of new life in Christ with me every day of our lives together.

Table Of Contents

Foreword

At the end of one of the earliest written testimonies of Christ's resurrection in the New Testament, Paul adds a very pastoral word.

Therefore, my beloved, be steadfast, immovable, always excelling in the work of the Lord, because you know that in the Lord your labor is not in vain.
— 1 Corinthians 15:58

Troubled though he was by the congregation in Rome, Paul loved them deeply. And he clearly wanted them to know Christ's resurrection not solely as a one-time wonder but as the basis for faithful and productive living. Because Christ was raised, they could live knowing that their fidelity to Christ was not in vain.

Later in his letter to the Christians in Rome, he makes the point even more dramatically. In baptism, says Paul, we have been buried with Christ, and we know that if we have been joined with him in death we shall also be joined with him in the resurrection. (Romans 6:5) In Christ, we "have been brought from death to life." (Romans 6:13)

In this collection of sermons we see another pastor seeking to remind his congregation of the significance of Christ's resurrection for their daily walk. He selects Jesus' parables as clues to the resurrected life Christians are enabled to live. The parables, the most characteristic form which Jesus' teaching took, reveal ordinary life as it is transfigured by the arrival of God's Reign. In experiencing what it is like for an alienated son to return home or for the later arrivals at work to be given a whole day's wage we experience within a characteristic of God's Reign. The parables become proclamations of possibility in a world in which God reigns and Christ is raised victorious from the grave.

The author has made imaginative use of contemporary parable and story to illustrate that God's presence is made known in the common circumstance of life. The intermixture of biblical parable and contemporary story helps to illustrate how the daily round is illuminated by the light of the resurrection.

I invite your meditation on these messages and trust that all of us may find in them tangible guides for the living of these days.

Neal F. Fisher, President
Garrett-Evangelical Theological Seminary

Preface

The inspiration for this series of sermons comes from a book by Neal Fisher titled *The Parables of Jesus: Glimpses of God's Reign.* Dr. Fisher is now president of Garrett-Evangelical Theological Seminary and was associate dean of Boston University School of Theology during my years of study there. I have always appreciated his inspiration and encouragement in my work.

President Fisher's book essentially argues that the parables in the gospels point to a New Age inaugurated by the coming of Jesus Christ, and that they "unveil a future which is already making an impact on the present."[1]

In the ministry, death and resurrection of Jesus Christ, we receive a glimpse of the life and age to come. It is true, as Dr. Fisher argues, that God's reign began before the resurrection with the appearance of Jesus Christ as the Word made flesh. However, the resurrection is the fullest expression of that expectation, the assurance that the individual believer who accepts Christ as Lord and Savior has entered into the life eternal.

The resurrection of Jesus Christ marks the defeat of death and the entrance into eternal life with God. Eternal life is understood to be not only a future reality, but is life lived in harmony with God here and now.

The theme of these sermons is that in the parables of Jesus we receive glimpses of how God wants and expects us to live in the resurrection age. The parables demonstrate in a concrete and specific way the very heart and mind of the God revealed in Jesus Christ. To live our lives in the way defined by the parables is to live the life eternal. It is for this reason that the central idea of these proclaimed words is that of hope.

I begin with a sermon for Easter Day, which celebrates the inauguration of a new way and quality of life lived in the Spirit of God. The six sermons which follow are based on selected parables which grant us glimpses of eternal life itself, and

9

suggest ways in which we can more fully participate in God's great gift of eternal life.

My hope is that they may provide for the season of Easter a fresh alternative to sermons based on the common lectionary. I am grateful to those persons who have helped me in developing the theme and content of this book. Special appreciation is expressed to the people of Wesley United Methodist Church in New Castle, Pennsylvania, for their inspiration and support in preaching. As always, I am most grateful to my wife Pamela, who is my best and most honest critic, as well as my faithful partner in ministry.

Donald William Dotterer
New Castle, Pennsylvania

[1]Neal F. Fisher, *The Parables of Jesus: Glimpses of God's Reign,* (New York: Crossroad, 1990), p. 3.

Easter Sunday
John 20:1-18

Living In The Resurrection Age

*Let us pray: On this day, O God, we lift up our heads
and shout the good news that your son Jesus Christ is
risen from the dead. In these moments, may we come to
know in our hearts as well as our minds that Jesus lives
now and forever.*

*May the words of our mouths, the meditations of our
hearts, be acceptable in thy sight, O Lord our strength
and our Redeemer. Amen.*

Columnist Philip Yancey, in an article titled "A Russian
Resurrection," writes of his visit in October 1991 to the former
Soviet Union. He says that it "would be hard to overstate the
chaos that he found when he arrived in the Soviet Union, a
nation that was about to shed its historical identity as well as
its name."

Yancey reports that one day the central bank ran out of
money. Several days later the second largest republic withdrew
from the union. There was a sense of crisis everywhere.

Doctors announced that the best hospital in Moscow might
close its doors for lack of money. Crime was increasing near-
ly 50 percent a year. No one knew what the country would
be like in a year or even six months. Who would be responsi-
ble for controlling the nuclear weapons? Who would print the
money?

Certainly this once great empire was in confusion and tur-
moil. And yet Yancey found something else in his visit to Russia
in the midst of chaos and financial hardship. An attractive
young woman who was in charge of cultural affairs summed
up the new attitude in Russia toward Christianity.

This Russian woman said softly but with great emotion: "We have all been raised on one religion: atheism. We were trained to believe in the material world, and not in God. In fact, those who believed in God were frightened. A stone wall separated these people from the rest."

Then she said, "Suddenly we have realized that something was missing. Now religion is open to us, and we see the great eagerness of young people. We must explore religion, which can give us a new life, and a new understanding about life."

There are now Russian language Bibles on display in the Kremlin government building. The church bells are sounding again, and the churches are full of worshipers. Women in babushkas are publicly kneeling in prayer outside the great cathedrals, an act that just a few short years ago would have required great courage.

So it is. Here is a genuine miracle of God in our time. As Philip Yancey concludes, here, in the former Soviet Union, which was officially atheistic until 1990, here in perhaps the least likely of all places, here were the unmistakable signs of an authentic spiritual awakening.[1] Here were the signs of spiritual resurrection.

I believe that the road to faith in Jesus Christ begins when we come to the same realization that the young Russian woman had. We come to Christ, we seek out Christ in his holy church, when we realize that something is missing in our lives. We come today and every Sunday to this house of God to learn about this man Jesus Christ, for he is the one who can give us both a new life, and a new understanding about the meaning and significance of the lives we live.

What is it about this Jesus that enables us to find our purpose in living? Is it not, as the Russian people are discovering, that in the faith of our fathers and mothers we find a spiritual strength and power that is permanent? As the letter to the Hebrews tells us, "Jesus Christ is the same yesterday, today and forever." People still yearn for a solid spiritual foundation for their lives that has stood the test of time. It is for all those who seek this renewal of faith that the bells of Easter toll this day.

It is then the permanent and eternal nature of faith in Christ that is a spiritual anchor for people in all ages and places. For those who confess this faith in the eternal Christ, it is possible to say that we are living in the Resurrection Age. The empty tomb marks a new era in human history and consecrates the possibility of a new beginning for all of us. It demands a new way of living — a way of living in hope and peace, in love and justice.

The gospels make it very clear that Jesus was always looking forward to this resurrection. Early in his ministry, Jesus said that the temple of his body would be raised up in three days. (John 2:19-22) Indeed, it is possible to view the teachings of Jesus as instructive in the ways that we should live in this coming age, which would be inaugurated by his resurrection from the dead.

The stone rolled away from the empty tomb on Easter Day is such a sign for us. It is indeed God's greatest miracle. We Christians are Easter people, and we are compelled by fact and moved by faith to find our greatest joy in this the greatest event and mystery in all of human history.

Yes, the resurrection of Jesus Christ from the dead is God's greatest miracle. It is not great simply because a murdered man was raised from the dead. We remember that Jesus also raised his friend Lazarus from the dead as an act of love and mercy.

No, what is significant about the resurrection of Jesus Christ from the dead is that this was God's way of telling us that death is not the final word in life. That is the sign for our time, the sign for all of time.

When he raised Lazarus, Jesus said, "I am the resurrection and the life." The resurrection is our assurance that through Jesus Christ we find joy and peace of eternal life, that is, life lived in harmony with God now and forever.

Death is not the final word in life! We need not fear the grave because in Jesus Christ our souls will live forever. That is the everlasting hope and salvation we receive this day. The resurrection is the answer to our question, "What is missing in our lives?"

Having received this sign and this assurance, we are set free, once and for all time. But what are we set free to do, you might ask?

What we are set free to do is to choose life rather than death. That is the challenge of Easter for the Christian believer. What Easter does is invite us to reflect upon the ways in which we can witness better to the possibilities of new life which we encounter in our homes, at work, at school, and at church.

What the world needs now more than ever is the witness of our Easter faith. Nations, communities and individual people are seeking ways to get through the Good Fridays of their lives to the time of resurrection and new life.

What people need now more than anything else is a reason to hope. They need to be able to choose life rather than death. Jesus Christ gives us that ability to choose life, as he brings hope to each and every human being.

Joyce Hollyday tells the story of a school teacher who was assigned to visit children in a large city hospital who received a routine call requesting that she visit a particular child.

The teacher took the boy's name and room number, and was told by the teacher on the other end of the line, "We're studying nouns and adverbs in this class now. I'd be grateful if you could help him with his homework, so he doesn't fall behind the others."

It wasn't until the visiting teacher got outside the boy's room that she realized that it was located in the hospital's burn unit. No one had prepared her to find a young boy horribly burned and in great pain.

The teacher felt that she couldn't just turn around and walk out. And so she stammered awkwardly, "I'm the hospital teacher, and your teacher sent me to help you with nouns and adverbs."

This boy was in so much pain that he barely responded. The young teacher stumbled through his English lesson, ashamed at putting him through such a senseless exercise.

The next morning a nurse on the burn unit asked her, "What did you do to that boy?"

Before the teacher could finish her outburst of apologies, the nurse interrupted her: "You don't understand. We've been very worried about him. But ever since you were here yesterday, his whole attitude has changed. He's fighting back; he's responding to treatment. It's as if he has decided to live."

The boy later explained that he had completely given up hope until he saw the teacher. It all changed when he came to a simple realization. With joyful tears, the boy said: "They wouldn't send a teacher to work on nouns and adverbs with a boy who was dying, would they?"[2]

This wonderful story invites us to celebrate the gift of life even when all we seem to see around us is pain and disappointment and brokenness. It shows us that on the other side of pain, there is resurrection. It reminds us of what is possible whenever there is hope.

As men and women living in the modern world, we too need signs of hope and resurrection. We need the assurance that God is with us always. That is the promise we receive on Easter Day. We can have hope, because we are living in the Resurrection Age.

A child asks her mother, "Where is God?" Her mother answers, "God is everywhere." The child cries out, "But I want God to be somewhere!" So do we! We want God to be here, with us now and forever.[3] This is, I think the greatest significance of our Easter celebration. For Easter is the promise we receive that Christ lives, and he is among us even now. The resurrection story is the foundation of our hope that Christ lives in eternity and that we will live with him now and forever.

We should never underestimate the strength and the hope that God's presence can bring to our lives. Have you heard the story of the man whose hobby was growing roses? When he worked in his rose garden, he always whistled. It seemed to everyone that he was whistling much louder than was needed for his own enjoyment.

One day a neighbor asked him why it was that he always whistled so loudly. The man then took the neighbor into his home to meet his wife. The woman was not only an invalid, but was completely blind as well.

15

The man, you see, was whistling, not for his benefit, but rather for the benefit of his wife. He wanted his blind wife to know that he was nearby, and that she was not alone.

That story is a wonderful illustration of the significance of Easter Day. The affirmation that "Christ is risen" suggests that God is near to us. It reminds us that there is something stable, something permanent in creation that will not be defeated by human sin and evil. The empty tomb is our assurance that God stands in and behind our world, and that God is there to strengthen and uphold anything that is good.

The truth of the matter is that God in his great love and concern for us does not give us signs, miracles if you want to call them that. God gives us signs of his presence and work in the ordinary events of our everyday lives. Think of the birth of a child; reflect upon a Sunday school teacher's commitment and enthusiasm for sharing the gospel.

Think about the joy one feels upon coming home after leaving for a period of time. Consider how one is moved, staying to the end with another human being through hours of pain and dying.

These are the signs, yes, the miracles of God in our everyday lives. In each one of them, one senses the presence of hope, and the victory of eternal life over death. In these experiences, one really does feel the power of resurrection.

My brothers and sisters in Christ, as we confront the ultimate question of life and death which we all must face as individuals, we need the assurance of Easter. For you see, Good Friday and Easter go together. Because every person has some dark moments, some disappointments throughout the course of a lifetime.

And that is why we all need Easter, the day on which we celebrate God's greatest miracle. We need Easter as the assurance of a power that is beyond ourselves. We need Easter so that we may have hope for the future.

Because in the end, all human beings must face their death alone. We need Easter, with its hope for better days ahead in this life. We need the promise of life eternal which only Jesus Christ can bring us.

Most of you know the name of the great Christian hymn-writer Ira Sankey, who wrote "The Ninety and Nine" and "I Am Praying for You." He lived in Brooklyn, New York during the last years of his life. After years of blindness, he died in 1908.

Just before his death, in his blindness and his frailty, he dictated this farewell message: "I have only a little longer of earthly darkness, and then the sunshine of the Father's throne. God is love. Good night, good night."[4]

Those words by a man who left forever his mark on earth by writing great hymns of praise to God tell us something very important about why we have gathered here this Easter Day to celebrate the risen Christ. For Ira Sankey's blind eyes could see God when it mattered the most, as he was passing from this life into the life immortal. He had learned through a lifetime of praise and service to his Lord, that Jesus Christ is that missing piece in human life, and that in the end, God is all that matters.

Hallelujah, Hallelujah! Christ is risen, Christ is risen today! My prayer to you this glorious Easter morning is that you take this message with you and live with it every day of your life, as Christ lives in you. May God bless you all this Easter Day.

Benediction: Our Lord and our God, we have heard your word and praised your name for raising Jesus from the dead. As we go from this place, may he live in our hearts now and into eternity.

The blessing of God the Father, Son and Holy Spirit, be with you now and forever. Amen.

---

[1]Philip Yancey, "A Russian Resurrection," *World Vision,* April/May 1992, pp. 2-5.

[2]Joyce Hollyday, *Sojourners,* March 20, 1986, p. 19.

[3]Illustration by Donald J. Shelby, *Meeting the Messiah* (Nashville: The Upper Room, 1980), p. 20.

[4]*Pulpit Helps,* May, 1992.

The Return Of The Lost

Let us pray: Gracious and eternal Father, today we come seeking to understand your purpose and your will for our lives. Help us to know that although we seek you, you have sought us first in love. Lord, grant us wisdom in these moments. In Jesus' name we pray, Amen.

One of the most common complaints that I hear about the medical profession is that many doctors are too detached from their patients. People tell me that doctors don't have time to listen to them because they are so anxious to get on to the next patient. They say, "The doctors are all business these days."

Bruce Shragg, a radiologist in California, expresses his feelings toward his job of reading X-rays and determining the results of biopsies on his patients. It is very interesting, I think, to get the physician's perspective on this problem.

Dr. Shragg learns that a patient named Mrs. Chambers would be coming in for a biopsy. The doctor has been informed by a lab technician that the C.T. scan has shown a growth on her pancreas.

As the doctor makes his way toward the room where the biopsy will be performed, he says that many thoughts are running through his mind. He is thinking about his upcoming trip to the ocean, last night's dinner with a friend, and the new tires he needs for his car. Dr. Shragg admits that he isn't really thinking about the needle he is about to stick into his patient's abdomen.

The doctor walks into Mrs. Chambers' room and greets her with a smile. The woman is about 50, and appears fairly healthy and robust. As he performs the procedure, Dr. Shragg jokes with the woman. He says, "This won't hurt me a bit," as he tries to be funny.

But the doctor knows very well that there is nothing funny at all about what he is doing. He does his work quickly, hoping that the job will soon be done.

It took the lab pathologist about 10 minutes to process the results of the biopsy. He said that the test was a good one. The results were clear and unmistakable. The tumor was malignant cancer.

Dr. Shragg writes that for just a moment, he felt a sense of excitement because he had been able to make the correct diagnosis. But as he sauntered back to his office, he reminded himself that this woman had just been given a sentence of death.

The doctor says that he felt relief that he would not be the one to tell this woman that she had cancer. He felt conflicting emotions of guilt and accomplishment. Yes, he had exercised good judgment and skill. He had done his job and done it well.

And wasn't this all that a doctor could hope to do? "Yes," he thought to himself, "a degree of detachment" was necessary in order for him to perform his duties effectively.

Then Dr. Shragg thought again of his patient, Mrs. Chambers. He considered how she would soon be faced with putting her affairs in order, how she would have to say good-bye to her two sons and her two-year-old granddaughter.

And with a sense of guilt, all the doctor could do was pick up his microphone, begin reading X-rays, and dictating the results.[1]

Isn't it true that in order for us to survive in life, we must operate with a "degree of detachment?" We might ask, just how can we survive if we cannot detach ourselves emotionally from the pain and suffering which we encounter every day?

A fireman must fight a fire without breaking down in tears over the person who is trapped inside. A policeman must make an arrest of a young and misguided man, realizing that the result will be a criminal record, thus making the boy a marked man, destined to live a life of rejection. A businessman may have to fire a likable, but unproductive worker in order to keep the company profitable and other people employed.

And even those of us who do not work in professions which require a degree of emotional detachment find that we must somehow keep our distance if we are going to be able to cope with the problems of friends and relatives.

Because, yes, it is very difficult to stay closely involved with people who are alcoholics. We may even find ourselves unable to stay close to a friend or relative who has a debilitating illness. Sometimes even immediate family members do not talk about serious problems among themselves, let alone with friends or extended family.

And this attitude of detachment is even easier to practice when we are confronted with issues that do not touch us personally. We may feel badly about the unemployment and poverty in our community, but if it does not touch us personally, we probably will not try to do very much about it.

Of even less concern are starving children in Africa or the working conditions of migrant farm workers. They simply do not attract very much of our attention. And so we remain detached and aloof, responding only to those needs which touch us personally.

It seems obvious that modern-day Americans are people who are becoming more and more isolated from one another. Columnist Paul Craig Roberts calls the United States a nation that is reverting to feudalism. He writes, "Neighborhoods in famous American cities, such as Miami and Los Angeles, are walling themselves off by erecting gates across public streets .... Increasingly, new housing developments are designed as walled enclaves. There are now more private security guards than public police officers."[2]

I believe that Jesus' well-known and much loved parable about the Good Shepherd gives us some important insight into this matter of distance and detachment. It is helpful for us to consider the background of this parable, so that we might understand its application to our personal lives.

Jesus addressed this parable to the Pharisees, that group of Jewish men who claimed the interpretation of God's law to be their professional responsibility. The Pharisees were shocked by the fact that Jesus would associate with people whom they had designated as the official "sinners" of the community. It was the deliberate policy of the Pharisees not to associate with those who did not observe the smallest details of the Jewish law.

It was bad enough that Jesus spoke to such people as tax-collectors — it was unforgivable that he would eat and socialize with them. Such behavior would religiously defile any upstanding, law-abiding Jewish citizen.

And so in order to address social rejection of the common people, Jesus told the parable of the lost sheep. He tells this story in defense of his ministry to the sinners and tax collectors.

In Jesus' time, the work of a shepherd was difficult and dangerous. Good grazing areas were scarce, and the steep cliffs which dropped off the region's central plateau were a constant threat to the well-being of the sheep. There were no fences or barriers to keep the sheep from tumbling over the hillside and into the desert below.

One hundred sheep were considered to be a good-sized flock in those days. The shepherd was personally accountable for every one of his sheep. He could tell each one apart by its face and personality. Any shepherd worth his salt would not hesitate to risk life and limb in order to save a single lamb that found itself in danger.

The image of a shepherd carrying a sheep safely home on his shoulders is a familiar symbol in Jewish history. Furthermore, in the book of Isaiah, God is described as one who "will feed his flock like a shepherd; he will gather the lambs in his arms, and carry them in his bosom, and gently lead the mother sheep." (Isaiah 40:11)

The point that Jesus is making with his parable is this: God our Father in heaven is like the good shepherd who would leave his 99 sheep to find the one that has gone astray. The message here is that there is no limit to the distance that God will go to bring us home to his love. For you see, God also knows the joy of finding and bringing home that which is lost.

Certainly this is good news for us, people who so often feel lost and alone in a difficult and confusing world. As Edward Carothers observes, this parable illustrates very well for us Jesus' belief that, with God's help, our lives can move from bad to good, from hurt to healing, from death to life. "His own personal experience of God led him to see in this process the active work of God. This is the kingdom of God! God acts now to save the lost and redeem the times, provided, in all situations, there is the acceptance of judgment."[3]

The teaching here then is that God does not operate with "a degree of detachment" from us. God is not, as the popular song says, "watching us from a distance." No, instead, God our loving Father is right here among us. He is closer to us than the air we breath. God is within us, loving us, feeling our pain, and desiring that we be made whole and happy and healthy people.

Likewise, God wants us as his created children to care for one another as he cares for us. God does not desire that we live our lives detached and aloof from the pain and brokenness of other people. This is how we as disciples of Jesus should live in this new age inaugurated by the life, death, and resurrection of our Lord and Savior.

Four people, one writer and three businessmen, were sitting at a dinner table with Bishop Desmond Tutu, the 1984 Nobel Peace Prize winner and great advocate for racial equality in South Africa. As they sat finishing their dessert, one of the men asked the bishop, who has done so much in the name of justice, what they could do to promote world peace.

Bishop Tutu gazed into the distance, thought for a moment, and then answered in a quiet voice. He said simply, "You must care."[4]

That is a very simple answer from a man of great accomplishment and a man of great Christian faith. One might have expected him to speak of organizing demonstrations, of registering people to vote, or of boycotting companies that produce weapons of war and destruction. But no, that comes later. First of all one must care in one's heart.

It is like the story about a little boy who strayed from the farmhouse one night. It was a damp and dark evening, and the toddler simply wandered out of the open door of the house. He was probably gone an hour before he was missed.

When his mother went to find him, she called his name, but there was no answer. She looked everywhere for the lost child — upstairs, downstairs, in the cellar. At last she realized that the child had gotten out of the house. The mother ran into the barnyard, where the men were finishing their chores. But to no avail. The little boy had not been there.

In that particular rural area there were huge wheat fields in all directions. The local residents organized a search party. But it was so dark and rainy that they soon had to give up the search.

At daybreak the next morning a larger search party went out again. Frustrated by the lack of success, one man called everyone together and said: "This is crazy. We're running every which way without any plan or organization or attempt to work together. That child could be one or two yards away from you in that tall wheat and you wouldn't notice him. Why don't you just line up, hold hands, and move in a straight line?"

That is just what they did. Thirty or 40 yards away they found the little boy. He had fallen into a gully, and had been drifting in and out of consciousness all night. The searchers picked the child up and rushed him back to the farmhouse.

The mother was sitting on the doorstep with the people looking on. The lost child was placed into the mother's arms. With tears streaming down her face, she cried: "My God, what would have happened if you waited any longer to hold hands?"[5]

My friends in Christ, it is time indeed for us to hold hands. Let us wait no longer to join together in this church and in this community to love one another as God our Father in heaven has loved us. As God has forgiven us, we must forgive and forget no matter how hard that is to do.

Wherever there is conflict between individuals, wherever there is pain and suffering, we need to put our differences aside and be united in our common purpose: to help build the kingdom of God on earth.

Yes, it is time for us to stop being detached and aloof and avoiding one another. It is time to join hands in Jesus Christ to build a better world. Because this is the only way for those who have been lost to experience the joy of being found.

May God bless you all as you seek the Lord Jesus in all that you do. May you know the peace of Christ in your heart this day.

> *Benediction: Gracious and loving Father, we have heard your word of life and sung praises to your name. We know what it means to be lost and then found. As we go from this place, let us proclaim that good news from the bottom of our hearts. Help us to care for one another in all that we do.*
>
> *Now may the peace of the Lord Jesus Christ, the love of God, and the fellowship of the Holy Spirit be with you now and always, Amen.*

---

[1] Bruce Shragg, "A Degree of Detachment," *New York Times Magazine,* July 26, 1987, p. 48.

[2] Paul Craig Roberts, "Nation Reverts to Feudalism," Scripps Howard News Service. Published in the *New Castle News,* December 15, 1992, p. 4.

[3] J. Edward Carothers, *Living with the Parables: Jesus and the Reign of God* (New York: Friendship Press, 1984), p. 16.

[4] *Daily Guideposts, 1986* (Carmel, New York: Guideposts Associates, 1985), p. 244.

[5] Thomas F. Reese, "Time to Hold Hands," *The Living Church,* September 15, 1991, p. 11.

Easter 3
Luke 14:28-33

Counting The Cost

Let us pray: O God of love and glory, on this day we come to you asking that your Spirit might be with us as we consider the important decisions in life that we all must make. Lord, in these moments, may we feel your presence among us. In Jesus' name we pray, Amen.

The major issue of the 1992 presidential campaign was the state of the American economy. Bill Clinton, George Bush and Ross Perot all offered different solutions to the problems of stalled economic growth and unemployment. It was the American people's deep sense of uneasiness over what economist Adam Smith would call "the wealth of the nation" that ultimately prompted them to vote for a change in our national leadership.

The campaign was unusual in some respects, but similar to other presidential elections in one significant way. As a major weekly magazine suggested, rarely did the candidates offer "a sustained emphasis on healing the country or forging a consensus for sacrifice." The main reason is that the question, "What's in it for me?" has a higher priority for most voters than healing or sacrifice.

James Wall of the *Christian Century* has noted this, and observed that the general tone of the debate in that campaign was that of selfishness. I believe that this observation could be applied to elections at all levels over the past 20 years. Wall comments that we "do not expect our presidential candidates to be frank either about 'sacrifice' or 'fairness,' at least not until after November 3. That is the sad, but realistic state of our democracy."

However, while the words "sacrifice" and "fairness" are rarely heard in political campaigns, they must be heard in the governing of the nation. As Mr. Wall suggests, the churches can play a role in making this happen. He argues against those who think that religion must be restricted politically to the realm of private moral decision-making.

He uses this example to help us understand the dilemma. Two thousand years ago, in the time of Christ, a regular assignment for a Roman schoolboy would be to write an essay. In that essay he would be asked to think of himself as an historical person at a time of economic and political crisis. Marius among the ruins of the ancient city-state of Carthage in North Africa was a favorite subject.

This would be like asking one of our youth here at the church to write an essay on the German bombing of England during World War II. This exercise was not only a good way to teach history, but it forced the schoolboy to place himself both outside and inside the character of another person in another place and time in history.

Mr. Wall believes that the proper role of religion is to fight against the struggle of selfish interests. True religion should fight against the perspective that nothing but the private self exists, and that life is a Hobbesian struggle of selves against each other. The question, "What's in it for me," is the end result of that philosophy of life.

On a much deeper level, true religious feeling encourages us to respond to God's identification with our pain and the pain of others. Furthermore, religion should help us to empathize with the pain of others. Because it is through this caring for the pain and suffering of others that we can rise above the debilitating limits that selfishness places upon us.

If we try to view the world from the perspective of another person, as the Roman schoolboy was asked to do, then we can discover the importance of sacrifice and fairness, and begin to appreciate its fundamental role in the foundation of democracy and of our country.[1]

I found this essay titled "The Language of Sacrifice" to be very interesting as I reflected upon the scripture lesson for the morning. Because what Jesus' parables of the tower builder and the king contemplating a military campaign are all about is the willingness of men and women to make sacrifices in order to gain that which is greater, that which is most precious in life.

Jesus asks his audience this question: "Who among you would begin to build a tower without first estimating the cost of completing it?" The tower of which Jesus spoke was most likely a vineyard tower. Vineyards in those days were often equipped with towers from which guards could protect the harvest from thieves who might steal the grapes.[2]

The point of the parable is that the wise man will carefully consider whether or not his resources are sufficient to complete a building before he lays the foundation. The man who does not do this runs the risk of being ridiculed and regarded as a failure in life.

The image of an unfinished structure was a familiar one to Jesus' audience. Indeed, even today, what is more embarrassing than a building that has not been completed, a job left unfinished? Perhaps you have heard the jokes about the infamous "Bridge to Nowhere" in Pittsburgh. In the community where we lived prior to coming to this appointment, people would shake their heads as they drove past a proposed parking area that one church started, but lacked the funds to finish.

Yes, when we think about it, things left unfinished in life can cause us great pain and sadness. That is why we are saddened when a young man or woman's life is cut short by illness or accident before the biblical three score and 10 years. It is sad because we know that this is a life that has not been completed. This is why we almost always consider an early death to be a tragedy, while dying at an advanced age is often considered a blessing. And this is perhaps what causes the greatest pain in divorce — because something good that was started in love has not been completed and fulfilled.

So it is. As Jesus' teaching reminds us, anything that is worthwhile in life has a cost. There is indeed a high price to be paid for anything that is really worth having. There must be sacrifice. There must be a fairness that requires the giving up of our selfish inclinations. In order to live life fully and happily, we must be people who are able to count the cost in almost every area of living.

Marriage is one of those institutions which demands a high personal cost. The church's wedding ritual begins with these sobering words, words that are so often taken too lightly. It says, marriage is "not to be entered into unadvisedly, but reverently, discreetly, and in the fear of God." Each person makes a covenant to love, comfort, honor and take care of the other in sickness and in health. That can be a difficult commitment to keep if a spouse becomes critically ill or severely disabled. The husband and wife agree to stay with each other "for better, for worse, for richer for poorer . . . till death do us part." A man and woman must count the cost of what they are getting into in marriage.

So it is also with having children. Did you see a recent letter to Ann Landers in the paper? It struck a chord with this expectant father heading toward his 40th birthday. The writer was talking about the mixed blessings of raising children in your 40s and 50s. It is true, I think, that an older father is more patient, and in a way, more appreciative of children.

However, as this letter-writer rightly suggests, raising children at a later age is also more difficult in many ways. Men or women in their 40s and 50s generally have a lower energy level, so taking the kids to Little League, attending PTA meetings and so forth tires parents much more.

Indeed, there are tremendous physical, emotional, and financial costs to raising children. Before having them, a couple should count the cost. There are just too many lonely and neglected and deprived children out there with parents who have not done so.

In the scripture lesson, Jesus makes his point again with another illustration. He asks his audience, "What king, preparing to go to battle against another king, would not first sit down and consider whether or not his army of 10,000 men would be able to fight successfully against 20,000?"

This is the mistake that Saddam Hussein made against the Coalition of Nations, which opposed his invasion of Kuwait. Hussein was crushed, because he did not carefully count the cost of his aggression.

The point that Jesus is making in these parables is that the life of faith in God also has a price. As the great German theologian Dietrich Bonhoeffer has put it so directly, there is a "cost of discipleship." There is no such thing as "cheap grace." If we want to know God, and if we want to receive the gift of eternal life from his son Jesus Christ, then there are some things that we must do in order to gain these gifts.

The life of faith is one that demands sacrifice and fairness toward others. The life of faith means that we must once and for all renounce the curse of selfishness in our lives. This is the way that God expects us to live in the new age that has been inaugurated by the life, death, and resurrection of his son Jesus Christ.

A missionary by the name of Viv Grigg writes about his personal search for God. When Mr. Grigg was nine years old he had a dream about being a missionary in the Brazilian jungle. The next day, for a class "what-do-you-want-to-be-when-you-grow-up assignment," he wrote that he wanted to be, of all things, a missionary.

At age 16 Viv Grigg picked fruit in the summer to save money for his university education. He lived in a dormitory with the other workers, mostly poor alcoholics and prostitutes. The destitute people and back-breaking labor were in sharp contrast to his middle class life in Dunedin, New Zealand. Yet instead of shrinking from his co-workers, Mr. Grigg loved them; he introduced them to Jesus Christ.

When he was 23 this remarkable young man fulfilled his dream and moved to Manila, the Philippines, where he spent his first term as a missionary. However, he was shocked to learn that many of his fellow missionaries lived in fancy homes, far removed from the slums of that city.

He knew that the Bible made it clear that the most effective way to reach the urban poor was to live among them, just as Jesus did. And so for the next 15 years Grigg helped to start churches in some of the most squalid cities on earth, including Manila, Calcutta and San Paulo.

Viv Grigg says this about the search for God. "Most people want the power of God but are not willing to walk the way of the cross. Knowledge of his power and the Holy Spirit is a very quiet thing that creeps up on those who work with the poor as God works with them. Work with the poor grants us the reward of walking with God."

Grigg acknowledges, of course, that not all people are called to live among the poor. But, he adds, "all Christians are called to a forsaking lifestyle and giving to the poor."[3] If we are truly seeking God, we will direct ourselves toward living lives of sacrifice, fairness and justice for all. In John 12:26, Jesus says, "Whoever serves me must follow me, and where I am, there will be my servant also. Whoever serves me, the Father will honor."

My friends in Christ, we are indeed called to give of ourselves to God and to other people. That is the central and most difficult teaching of the Bible. It is the way that God expects us to live in the Resurrection Age.

But although the costs of discipleship may be high, the good news is that even greater still are the rewards of a life of faith. Because our faith in Christ, which is expressed and nurtured in the church, is that which brings joy, peace and happiness to troubled hearts that are in search of purpose and meaning. It is our faith that opens the door to everlasting life. Our faith is indeed our hope both now and forever.

My prayer for you this day is that you may make your investment in a life of faith this day. May God bless you now and always with his love and his peace.

Benediction: Gracious and eternal God, we have come together this day as friends to worship you and praise your name. We have heard something of what you expect from us as your disciples. As we go from this place, may we take the hope and peace of Christ with us in all that we do.

The grace of the Lord Jesus Christ and the love of God and the fellowship of the Holy Spirit be with you now and always. Amen.

---

[1]James Wall, "The Language of Sacrifice," *The Christian Century,* October 14, 1991, pp. 891-92.

[2]William Barclay, *The Gospel of Luke* (Philadelphia: Westminster Press, 1975), p. 197.

[3]Viv Grigg with Tamera Marko, "Living Among the Poor," *World Vision,* October/November 1992, pp. 19-20.

Easter 4
Matthew 18:23-35

The Condition Of Mercy

*Let us pray: Our Father and our God, on this day
we give you thanks for all the blessings of our lives. In
these moments, may we learn something about what it
is for which we need to be most thankful. Lord, in these
moments may we experience your mercy and your grace.
In Jesus' name we pray, Amen.*

A social psychologist by the name of David Myers has written a book titled *The Pursuit of Happiness*. The book has 59 pages of references and a 43-page bibliography. This large number of citations clearly demonstrates that many people have had much to say on that elusive subject called "happiness."

The central question that Dr. Myers poses is this one: Who is happy, and why are they happy? He then frames the question in a more detailed way: "What traits of personality, what circumstances of life, what states of mind correlate with well-being — with that joyful, and joy-spreading spirit that enables one to sense that simply being alive is the most wonderful of life's gifts?"[1]

This psychologist argues that happiness has remarkably little to do with age, gender, race, location, education, wealth, personal tragedies, or social standing. However, it does have a lot to do with physical health, self-esteem, optimism, engaging work, and supportive friends and family.

Then Dr. Myers poses the question that is important for us as a religious community: What does faith have to offer to the state of being happy? In the Christian context, faith expressed in the church of Jesus Christ offers first of all a caring community. You are well aware that in most churches there is an outpouring of love and support when illness or tragedy strikes a family.

Furthermore, faith offers us the belief that God our Creator accepts us just the way we are, the way he made us. Faith in Christ offers a call to unselfish living, and a perspective on dying that enables us to face death without fear. It is our belief in eternal life that enables us to believe that human life has value and significance.

Therefore you might say that our faith offers something to live for, and something to die for.

There is, I think, one more contribution which faith has to offer us in our search for happiness in human life. It is that condition which Jesus talked about in his parable of the "Two Debtors." It is about what we might call "the condition of mercy."

Jesus tells the story of a king who was settling his accounts with his slaves. He called before him one slave who owed him 10,000 talents. Now in those days this was an enormous debt. A rough equivalent would be $10 million in today's money.

The size of a 10,000 talent debt can be appreciated when we realize that Herod the Great had an annual income of 900 talents. The total annual tax for the regions of Galilee and Peraea in the year 4 B.C. was only 200 talents.[2]

Who knows what this man had done to incur such a debt. It would have to have been something comparable to the savings and loan scandal of the 1980s. The debt was so enormous that there was no possibility of the man ever repaying the loan to his master.

And so the king, seeing the magnitude of the debt, ordered that the slave, his wife, his children and all his possessions be sold. In those days, it was not unusual for persons to be sold into slavery to pay a debt. This would have made only token payment, but the king would have at least recovered some of his lost money.

However, the slave fell on his knees and begged for mercy from the king. He promised to repay the debt, an act that was, of course, impossible.

36

It is the response of the king that is important for us to appreciate. What he does here is immediately respond with more than the servant has asked. The king not only decides not to sell the man and his family into slavery, but to forgive entirely the enormous debt. The slave leaves the court as a free man.

We would perhaps like the parable to end here with a happy ending. However, now we get, as Paul Harvey says, "the rest of the story."

The one who is rescued from bondage now comes upon a fellow slave. This slave owed him 100 denarii. This amount would be approximately $1,000 in today's money. It was, of course, a very trifling amount when compared to the enormous debt which the first slaved owed to the king.

The first slave grabs his debtor by his neck, saying, "Pay what you own me." The fellow slave falls on his knees and pleads for patience and understanding. But the first slave refuses, throwing his debtor into prison.

His fellow slaves, who were greatly troubled by the injustice, then ran to the king to tell him what happened. The king called back the first slave, and literally bawled him out for his unmerciful behavior. Then the king has his debtor thrown into prison.

Jesus closes his parable with these words: "So my heavenly Father will also do to every one of you if you do not forgive your brother or sister from the heart."

So what is Jesus saying in this teaching? What really is the point of it all?

What this parable is about is the enormous capacity of God in heaven to forgive us, the children whom he has created in his very own image. It is about the unlimited nature of God's love. The truth revealed here is that there is nothing, nothing that we have done for which God cannot forgive us.

The fact is that our sins are lost in the sea of God's love and forgiveness. That is the one truth that all Christians, be they liberals or conservatives, evangelicals or moderates, Catholics or Protestants can agree upon.

Yes, our sins are lost once and forever in the love of God. All that we must do to receive the forgiveness of God is to say that we are sorry, and then try to do better.

The greatest news of the Christian gospel is that we do have this opportunity to start over if we are able to sincerely repent of wrongdoing. In the midst of our moral and spiritual failures, the crucifixion and resurrection of Jesus Christ assures us that the slate has been wiped clean, once and for all time. The Christian hope rests in the conviction that our future lies in still-to-be-seen future, rather than in a soiled and painful past. In Jesus Christ, there is always the opportunity to begin again through the simple but profound acts of our repentance and God's forgiveness.

However, the problem for the unmerciful slave was that he did not try to do better. He was willing to accept forgiveness as a gracious gift from his master, but he was not willing to do the same for somebody else.

What Jesus is saying here is that this is the kind of behavior that God cannot and will not tolerate. This parable is one of the most important teachings that Jesus ever shared. Because in this story Jesus is illustrating the principle which is enshrined in the Lord's Prayer which we say here every Sunday morning: that we are to forgive our debtors just as we have been forgiven by God our Father in heaven.

There is no question that it is not easy to forgive those who have wronged us. Some may have been cheated financially. But usually the offense is more personal. The anger we feel is rooted in our feelings of being humiliated, or having been used or taken advantage of in a careless and insensitive way. Often we feel that our pride has been wounded. Perhaps the offense is having had something that we love very dearly taken away from us.

Beulah Mae McDonald is a black woman who has earned a reputation as "The Woman Who Beat The Ku Klux Klan." On March 21, 1981, Mrs. McDonald had a dream in which she saw a steel-gray casket sitting in her living room. Every time she tried to move closer to the casket, someone told her, "You don't need to see this."

But Mrs. McDonald knew that she did have to see it. And when she awoke from her dream, the first thing she did was to look in the other bedroom where her youngest son Michael was supposed to be sleeping. He was not there.

When the boy didn't come home the next morning, Mrs. McDonald knew that something was wrong. The phone rang. The caller said, "They had a party here, and they killed your son. You better send somebody over." A few blocks away, in a racially mixed neighborhood, about a mile from the Mobile, Alabama, police station, they found Michael McDonald's body hanging from a tree. Around his neck was a perfectly tied noose with 13 loops.

On a front porch across the street, watching police gather evidence were members of the United Klans of America, one of the largest and most violent of the Ku Klux Klans. Looking across the street, Bennie Jack Hays, the 64-year-old Titan of the United Klans, said, "A pretty sight. That's gonna look good on the news. Gonna look good for the Klan."

The men who killed Beulah Mae McDonald's son thought they would go free. But they were wrong. Not only did the young black man's killer receive the death penalty, but Mrs. McDonald won a seven-million dollar lawsuit which broke the back of this hate group which is driven by the power of Satan.

Mrs. McDonald was a single mother who had to raise her children alone and in poverty. She says this about raising her children: "I wasn't able to get everything for them, but I let them know the value of things." Her method of childrearing was that of love and religion.

On Sunday morning, Mrs. McDonald would take her family to church in the morning and remain there all day. "I'm a strong believer," she explains. "I don't know about man, but I know what God can do."

It was the power of God that enabled Beulah Mae to do that which would have been impossible for an unbeliever. Her faith in God enabled her to forgive even those who had murdered her son.

At the civil trial, one of the Klansmen implicated in the crime named Tiger Knowles turned to Mrs. McDonald. They locked eyes for the first time. Knowles spoke of the seven million dollars which he and the others were going to have to pay as the consequence of their crime.

"I can't bring your son back," he said sobbing and shaking. "God knows if I could trade places with him, I would. I can't. Whatever it takes — I have nothing. But I will have to do it. And if it takes me the rest of my life to pay for it, any comfort it may bring, I hope it will." By this time, the jurors were crying. The judge had tears in his eyes.

Then Beulah Mae McDonald said these words: "I do forgive you. From the day I found out who you all was, I asked God to take care of y'all, and he has."[3]

Who among us could show that kind of forgiveness? The answer is, that none of us could ever do it without faith in God. Even with much smaller offenses, we cannot really and truly forgive without God's help.

One of the fundamental principles of Alcoholics Anonymous is that a person cannot stop drinking on one's own. The first step for the problem drinker is to acknowledge that he or she is out of control. Secondly, the person must seek spiritual help; one must petition the "higher power." With the help of God and participation in a supportive community, the demon of alcoholism can be defeated. However, the abuser cannot be delivered unless he or she truly wants to stay sober. The personal will to change is the critical factor.

So it is also with mercy and forgiveness. We need the touch of a Mighty Hand to do that which is impossible for humans. We need the strength of a higher power and the community of faith to be merciful and pure in heart. However, there is no use in asking God to help us unless we desire in the depths of our hearts to really and truly forgive those who have hurt us.

But with God's help we can forgive. We can go on. We can start over again, no matter what has happened to us. Such is the condition of mercy, such is the condition of love which

God has granted to us in living. It is one of the conditions that must be present for us to find happiness in living.

The resurrection of Jesus Christ on Easter Day has inaugurated a new age, the kingdom of God on earth. In this Resurrection Age we are called to do things that we cannot do through our own power and strength. One of the aspects of holy living in this new age is the ability to forgive even when we do not believe that forgiveness is possible.

Today, on this fourth Sunday of Easter season on which we celebrate the living Christ, I invite you as the people of God to reflect deeply upon the love of God for you. Think about how God can help you find peace and happiness by enabling you to do those things which you never thought you could do.

Let us then praise and give thanks to God for his love and mercy this day. May you continue to have a blessed and happy Easter season!

Benediction: Gracious and eternal God, we have worshiped you and given thanks for all that you have done. As we go from this place, may we and those we love walk with your Spirit now and forever.

Now may the Lord bless you and keep you, may the Lord make his face to shine upon you and be gracious unto you, the Lord lift up his countenance upon you, and give you peace. Amen.

[1]David G. Myers, *The Pursuit of Happiness,* reviewed by Philip Blackwell in *The Christian Century,* October 7, 1992, p. 876.

[2]Neal Fisher, *The Parables of Jesus: Glimpses of God's Reign* (New York: Crossroad, 1990), p. 101.

[3]"The Woman Who Beat the Klan," *New York Times Magazine,* November 1, 1987, pp. 26-39.

*Easter 5
Matthew 25:14-29
Galatians 6:7-10*

Life As An Investment

*Let us pray: Gracious and eternal Father, we come
before you this day seeking to make the most of the gifts
which you have given us in life. Lord, as we now hear
your word, may we learn how it is that we may serve you
with all that we are. Lord, in these moments, grant us
wisdom, understanding and peace. In Jesus' name we
pray, Amen.*

During the 1992 presidential campaign, one of the slogans
which we heard frequently was "invest and grow." The meaning of this phrase of course is that the government will make
investments through tax dollars which will revitalize the economy of the nation.

While driving home from a hospital visit on election day,
I heard a commentator on the radio suggest that the guiding
principle for our lives should not be government investment,
but rather "invest in yourself." From his perspective, this is
the only way that an individual can improve his or her personal economic well-being.

So no matter which political persuasion you adhere to, it
does appear that the principle of "investment" will be one of
the leading ideas of the 1990s. And rightly so, I think. For
it is through the spending of our time, talents, and money in
ways that lead to future productivity and growth that nations,
churches, and individual lives are improved and made more
meaningful and enjoyable.

It is quite natural then that Jesus would give a lesson on
what a businessman might call "investment principles." This
is the subject of Jesus' well-known teaching called the "Parable of the Talents."

43

This is the story. Jesus tells of a man who goes away on a long trip. While he is away, the man entrusts to his three servants different amounts of money.

The word used here is "talent," which meant in Jesus' time a specific weight of silver or gold. Each talent might have been worth about $1,000 in today's dollars. The modern use of the word "talent" with regard to skill or ability originated with this parable.

So the rich man gives the first servant five talents, the second servant two talents, and the third servant one talent. We are told that each servant is given an amount which is proportionate to his ability to handle the responsibility.

Apparently the man knew the ability of his servants very well. The first servant invested his money and doubled his investment. The second servant did the same with the lesser amount with which he had been entrusted.

However, the third servant proved his predicted incompetence to his master. Instead of investing his money like the others, he buried his treasure in the ground. This would be the equivalent of stuffing money in a mattress at home. This servant therefore did not even make the easy money that could be made by simply giving the money to the bankers.

When the master comes home, he of course expresses his happiness with the servants who had doubled his money. He said to them those words that we would all want to hear from our superiors, "Well done, good and trustworthy slave. You have been trustworthy in a few things, I will put you in charge of many things; enter into the joy of your master." These workers had earned a promotion in the company through their wise stewardship of the master's resources.

However, the master also expresses his extreme displeasure with the servant who buried the money in the ground. His one talent was taken away from him and given to the man who had the 10 talents.

The master's closing words, in effect, are these: "The person who has succeeded will always be given more; but he who has not invested what he has will have what he has been given taken away from him.''

Steven Jobs is the man who founded the enormously successful company called Apple Computer. Jobs decided that Mr. John Sculley was the man needed to help him fulfill his dream of building a completely different kind of computer company, one which would make computers available to every person in the world.

However, Mr. Sculley was comfortably and safely entrenched as president of the Pepsico Corporation, the makers of the soft drink Pepsi. In this position, John Sculley had achieved everything that a man could want — power, prestige, public recognition, an enormous salary and a secure future.

The thought of a career change requiring a move to the West Coast frightened him. He was concerned about losing pensions and deferred compensation and the adjustment to living in California — in other words, ''the pragmatic stuff that preoccupies the middle-aged.'' He says that ''I was overly concerned with what would happen next week and the week after next.''

John Sculley knew that he was safe and happy at Pepsico. But he also knew that he had grown to dislike the competitive nature of the business. He also knew how bored he was.

Steven Jobs at Apple Computer sensed this. And so he finally confronted his new friend with this pointed question. He said to John, ''Do you want to spend the rest of your life selling sugared water or do you want a chance to change the world?''

That question penetrated deep into the heart and mind of John Sculley. It changed the course of his life. He therefore went to Apple Computer and helped it to grow into one of the most successful corporations in the world. Mr. Sculley's life was changed because he took the risk and decided to invest in himself and others, and to grow.[1]

In the parable, Jesus had aimed his teaching at the religious establishment of the day, those scribes and Pharisees who did not want to see any growth or change in religion and faith. They were content to maintain the status quo, to keep things comfortable for themselves, not wanting to allow themselves or others to exhibit any spiritual growth.

Clearly then the message here is that we must be willing to invest and grow personally and spiritually. We must be people who are willing to take risks and open ourselves up to the creative movement of God's Holy Spirit in our lives. Unless we are able to do so, we will become stale and unproductive in our faith in Christ and service to his church and to his people.

It has been said that some persons do not know what is happening, while others watch what is happening. Other people wish that things would happen. There are still other people who hinder things from happening. And finally, there are those who make things happen.

This morning, as we consider this matter of investing and growing, we should ask ourselves: "Which category do you and I fall into?"

I am sure that you have heard of Helen Keller, that remarkable woman who was born blind and deaf. She became famous for her determination to learn to speak and read. She became a world-famous writer and lecturer as an advocate for handicapped persons.

Ms. Keller once said: "I long to accomplish a great and noble task, but it is my chief duty to accomplish tasks as if they were great and noble. The world is moved along, not only by the mighty shoves of its heroes, but also by the combined tiny pushes of each honest worker."[2]

These inspiring words from a truly great woman should encourage us to really want to make things happen. The things that we make happen do not have to be great in the eyes of humans. But that which we do to help build a better local community would and will indeed be considered important and significant by God our Father in heaven who knows all that we have done in his service.

So it is. To invest in yourself and others and to grow in faith is to make things happen in your life and in the lives of others. This is the key to making your life worth living.

There is another passage from the Bible which deals with this matter of life as an investment. It contains advice that Paul gave to the church at Galatia, words that have been called an "agriculture of the spirit."

In the sixth chapter of Paul's letter to the Galatians, he states what some might find to be a very hard truth. Yet despite the seriousness of his statement, it does represent what we might call the law of life. Paul is speaking here of a natural law which is ingrained in the very structure of the universe. The literal translation of Paul's words is this: "Do not be deceived; God is not mocked . . . ."

In other words, you may fool yourself and fool others into thinking that there are not consequences for your actions. But the truth is that God will not be fooled.

Paul then goes on to say, "For you reap whatever you may sow. If you sow to your own flesh you will reap corruption from the flesh; but if you sow to the Spirit, you will reap eternal life from the Spirit. So then, whenever we have an opportunity, let us work for the good of all, and especially for those of the family of faith."

Paul is saying that in the end, life holds the scales in an even balance. In the final analysis, there is a sort of Christian karma; we get exactly what we deserve in life, exactly what we have earned.

For example, if a person allows the dark and sinful side of his personality to control him, that person can expect nothing but a harvest of trouble. This is what Paul means when he speaks of "sowing to the flesh."

But on the other hand, if a person keeps walking in the way of the Spirit, then there will be rich rewards. We may have to wait a long time, and sometimes it may seem to be a terribly long time — but in the end, God will repay the person who is persistent in faith and good works, the person who had invested in himself, in others, and in the service of Christ.

Paul then encourages us to think of life as an investment rather than a gamble. The natural law created by God imposes a discipline upon us that encourages us to shape our lives in ways that are useful and productive.

I would guess that many of you in this congregation are gardeners, people whose gardens are evidence of the "green thumbs" in this church. But as all good gardeners know, there is really nothing mysterious about a "green thumb."

Having a green thumb is simply the practice of faithfully, you might say "religiously," cultivating and nurturing the seeds. If a good seed is planted in fertile ground and receives the right amount of sunlight and water, the gardener does not need to worry about the results. According to the laws of nature, the plant will flourish.

In the Bible, the image of a garden appears in many places. Two instances of special significance are the Garden of Eden and the Garden of Gethsemane. In both instances, the gardens represent places where God and humans meet, symbolizing an unbroken fellowship between the Father and his children.[3]

Do you not think, my friends, that life itself is much like cultivating a garden? As Lawrence Crumb suggests, we might say that there is a "garden of the human heart." "It is a place where the flowers of truth and goodness can blossom in all of their beauty if properly tended or where the weeds of sin can take over as a result of accidental or deliberate neglect."[4]

Why do once-promising marriages end in divorce? Why do friendships grow faint over the years? Why do persons fall away from the church and their faith in God?

The reason is simple. Our relationships with God and other people fail because they have not been nurtured and cared for well enough. Marriages and friendships involve an investment of time; they require sacrifice, hard work, and cultivation.

So it is also with the life of faith. We need to regularly worship and study the Bible. We must spend time in prayer talking to God our Father in heaven if our faith is to grow and develop into a source of strength and peace in living.

The garden of the human heart is a place where one can encounter God in perfect fellowship, but it is also where serpents of doubt and despair can rise up. It is a place where agonizing struggles and decisions take place, but it is also where angels come to minister to us when we need the touch of God's loving hand upon our lives.[5]

My friends in Christ, we are indeed called by God to invest in faith and to grow in love. In order to find peace and happiness in living, we must be people who are willing to make things happen in our individual lives, in our families, and in this church. In the new age which was inaugurated by the life and resurrection of Jesus Christ, we are called to see as an investment in our Lord and in his people.

Let our prayer this day then be that we be people who can grow in faith and love in all that we do. May God bless you all on your journey of faith.

Benediction: Gracious and eternal God, we have heard your word and praised your name. As we go from this place may we grow in faith and service in your name.

Go now to serve God and your neighbor in all that you do. May the peace of the Lord be with you always, Amen.

---

[1]John Sculley, *Odyssey* (New York: Harper & Row, 1987), p. 90.

[2]J. J. Turner quoting Helen Keller in *Pulpit Helps.*

[3]Lawrence N. Crumb, "God's Place in the Garden," *The Living Church,* April 12, 1992, p. 10.

[4]*Ibid.*

[5]*Ibid.*

Easter 6
Matthew 13:44-46

Surprised By Joy

Let us pray: O God our heavenly Father, in many ways we seek to know you so that we might find the true riches of life. Hear now thy servants who desire to learn of your love and glory. In the name of Jesus we pray, Amen.

The Christian author C.S. Lewis, in an autobiography which he has titled *Surprised by Joy,* tells of his conversion to Christianity. This book is an account of how Lewis, an accomplished and well-known British intellectual, became a truly Christian person. It is about leaving the superficial religion of his childhood, and his movement to a deep and abiding faith in the God revealed in Jesus Christ. You should really read this book, which is both an amusing and yet very profound account of how, as Lewis describes it, "God closed in on me."

Being a fierce free thinker and free spirit, prior to his conversion, Lewis wanted, above all things, not to be "interfered with." He says that he wanted "to call my soul my own." But, as Lewis learns, after he met God, he was not to be allowed to "play" at philosophy any longer.

After years of fighting his conversion, God finally conquered the soul of C.S. Lewis. Lewis says this about his transformation: "You must picture me alone in that room in Magdalen, night after night, feeling, whenever my mind lifted even for a second from my work, the steady, unrelenting approach of him whom I so earnestly desired not to meet. That which I had greatly feared had at last come upon me. In the Trinity Term of 1929 I gave in, and admitted that God was God, and knelt and prayed: perhaps that night the most dejected and reluctant convert in all of England." God simply said to this man, "I am the Lord; I am that I am."

Lewis concludes, "The hardness of God is kinder than the softness of men, and His compulsion is our liberation."[1] Once God comes to us, God cannot be refused. So it is, once we have tasted God, only God will do.

C.S. Lewis then describes his experience of the person Jesus Christ which came later, after his conversion to mere belief in God. He uses a single word that many people today do not often associate with an experience of Christ. He calls that which he experienced deep in his soul simply "joy."

One can say then that to experience Christ in the depths of one's heart, to be converted, is to be "surprised by joy." What is this joy? It is something that cannot be described in human words. It is a feeling of God's presence that is at once both greater and more profound than pleasure. As Lewis says, perhaps all pleasures are but a substitute for joy.

Joy is not a possession. It is instead found in the desiring of Christ. The thrill comes only when one's whole attention and desire are focused on this something which is other than ourselves, this Christ who is a personal savior. Real joy points to something other and outer, to something bigger and greater than that which is human. To experience joy is to catch a glimpse of the spiritual, of the eternal. Real joy then is that feeling that points toward God. To feel joy is to experience personally the living Spirit of God Almighty in one's heart and soul.

In our gospel lesson, Jesus tells a parable that illustrated for his audience the meaning of joy. Jesus says that the kingdom of heaven, which we all are seeking, is like finding treasure that has been buried in a field. In doing so, Jesus strikes a theme which has always had romantic interest for men and women.

Who among us has not as a child, or perhaps even as an adult, dreamed of finding buried treasure which would make us rich and happy? Many of the best-loved stories of our youth, such as Robert Louis Stevenson's *Treasure Island,* have had the search for buried treasure as their theme.

Today, searching for buried treasure still has that romantic interest. However, actually finding buried treasure is something that rarely happens. But in Israel, in the time of Jesus, things were quite different.

The reason for this was that in those days there were no banks in which ordinary people could store their money. One of the common ways of safely storing one's fortune during threatening times was to bury the coins in a location which was only known to the owner.

It was not unusual for the owner to die without revealing the location of his buried treasure. It was therefore not uncommon for there to be an unexpected discovery of a fortune, for instance, when a farmer was plowing his field. It was this accidental discovery of gold, silver, or jewels that Jesus compares to finding the kingdom of heaven.

Who among us would not be thrilled by finding buried treasure? The point of Jesus' teaching here is that there is a great joy in finding God that is not unlike that of finding a fortune.

Furthermore, the truth is that the finding of God brings a much deeper and lasting joy than the uncovering of buried gold could ever bring us. Indeed, this finding of God is worth giving up everything one has in order to have it, just as the finder of buried treasure will sell all that he has in order to buy the field in which he made the discovery.

This parable then is good news for those of us who search for depth and meaning in our lives. We need this word of hope which tells us that yes, it is possible to find a source of joy that can last for eternity.

Do we not need this word of hope now more than ever? A newspaper carried an article with this headline: "Poll Shows Americans Are Deeply Pessimistic." This Gallup poll revealed some interesting information. It shows that two out of three Americans believe that the United States is in a serious long-term economic, moral and spiritual decline. The poll reveals a pessimism that is breathtaking in its sweep and intensity.

A majority of people believe that a good education doesn't insure getting a good job. Four in ten say working hard doesn't guarantee fair treatment from an employer. Almost half say they don't think their views will be taken seriously even if they do participate in the political process.[2]

Of course, nobody needed to tell us this. We all know that things are not going very well in so many areas of America's social and economic life.

But nevertheless, we who call ourselves Christians should have hope. Because you see, we are the ones who can experience real joy in living. And the reason is that if we have that joy deep down in our heart that only Christ can bring us, then we will have the strength and courage to overcome any obstacles which life may throw in front of us. As Paul teaches us in the letter to the Philippians (4:13), we can do all things in Christ who strengthens you and me.

The source of joy for the person who has faith is not at the mercy of other people and outward circumstances. Happiness for the Christian is not determined by his surroundings and other human beings. This is why Jesus taught in the parables that the spiritual treasure which God surprises us with is an inward and personal possession. Faith in Christ as Lord and Savior is God's gift to us in this resurrection age in which we live.

Gallia K. MacKinney writes in an article titled, "What I Discovered in Prison" about her conversion to Christianity. Her father was an operatic singer, her mother an artist. They lived on the French Riviera where they enjoyed the finer things of life — beautiful homes, servants, everything that money could buy. Ms. MacKinney says that she took it for granted that she deserved all this. The family motto was "All is ours. We have the money, we have the name, we have everything."[3]

However, all of that changed very quickly when World War II broke out and the occupation of France began. Gallia and her parents became involved in the resistance, aiding their Jewish friends who were trying to flee the country.

One day armed men came bursting into their home and arrested Gallia and her mother and father. They were taken to a confiscated hotel and questioned at gunpoint for hours.

Gallia and her parents were then separated. She was put onto a truck and taken away to a camp, which was actually a number of horsebarns with barbed-wire fences around them. It was filthy. She had to sleep on straw beds infested with lice. There was torture that was hard to describe.

One day after Gallia had returned from the medical compound where she had seen her mother, she saw a disheveled man get off one of the buses. Although it was strictly forbidden, she exchanged a few words with her father and passed messages on scraps of paper.

These brutalities could easily have broken Gallia, her mother and father. But one thing saved them. At different times, throughout their ordeal, Gallia, her mother and her father each accepted Jesus Christ as Lord and Savior. In him they found a joy that they had never had before, even in the happiest moments of their lives.

Finally, the Allied Forces arrived. The prison doors were opened, and Gallia and her parents were let out alive. They returned to their hometown.

Gallia MacKinney writes: "We had lost every earthly possession — money, furniture, jewelry, furs, clothes. Some Christians shared their ration cards with us until we were reestablished. Instead of a luxurious apartment, we now had two tiny rooms and we shared a public toilet between floors in the building. But we were happy."

She concludes her story with these words: "Many people fool themselves by saying, 'I bought it. It's mine.' But things can be taken away in the snap of a finger. It happened to Papa and Mama. It happened to me. But now I have everything. I have Christ. He can't be taken away."[4]

In the gospel lesson for the morning, Jesus reiterates his teaching by telling another parable. He says, "The kingdom of heaven is like a merchant in search of fine pearls; on finding one pearl of great value, he went and sold all that he had and bought it."

This parable is known as the "Pearl of Great Price." Its message is the same as that of the parable about buried treasure, except for one very important point. The pearl, for which the merchant would sell everything he has in order to own, is found only after a long and exhausting search. A merchant in search of fine pearls might travel as far as India or the Persian Gulf.[5]

So it is with our faith and trust in God. Faith in God is the only thing that matters in the end. It is indeed worth giving up everything we own in order to have this faith. And yet, it may not come in an instant.

Faith is something that we need to seek constantly in prayer and worship and study of God's Word. It is that which we must be willing to work and sacrifice for in order to receive. Faith is something that grows deeper and richer and more valuable to us with the passage of time.

There is a story about a prisoner in Sydney, Australia, who engineered a daring escape by climbing underneath the hood of a van delivering bread to a prison where he was serving his term. However, the escape was foiled when at the van's next stop, he climbed out hot and dirty, only to find himself in the yard of another prison, just four miles away from the one from which he had just escaped!

How often we seek escape from our unhappiness and boredom by moving from one situation to another, or from one person to another, or from one new purchase to another. It just seems characteristic of the human race to always be in search of some finer pearl.

We think that if we can find the right person, or rise to a certain level of income, this will bring us happiness. But those who believe that myth only find that enough is never enough. Some people go through their entire lives, always seeking a finer pearl, never being satisfied, escaping from jail to jail.

Deeper than the need for things is the need to be at peace with God and to trust in his will for our lives. Jesus Christ enables us to have that relationship with God that can bring us genuine happiness. It is what it means to be "surprised by joy." This is how God intended us to live in the new age inaugurated by his Son Jesus Christ.

My prayer for you is that you may find the peace of God and the joy of Christ in your heart this day and always. May you be blessed by God's Spirit in all that you do.

> *Benediction: Our Father and our God, we have worshiped together and shared the fellowship of the Holy Spirit. We have sought you in the depths of our hearts in prayer. As we go from your house, may you be with us in all that we do.*
>
> *May the blessing of God the Father, Son, and Holy Spirit be with you now and always, Amen.*

[1]C.S. Lewis, *Surprised By Joy* (New York: Harcourt, Brace & World, Inc., 1955), pp. 227-228.

[2]*Youngstown Vindicator*, September 13, 1992, p. C-1.

[3]Gallia K. MacKinney, "What I Discovered in Prison," *Wondrous Power Wondrous Love* (Minneapolis: World Wide, 1983), p. 212.

[4]*Ibid.*

[5]*Interpreter's Bible,* vol. 7, p. 420.

Easter 7
Matthew 20:1-16

Surprised By Grace

Let us pray: Gracious and eternal Father, we come
to you this day seeking to understand the ways in which
your Spirit moves in our lives. Lord, in these moments,
may we be moved by love in our hearts and receive wis-
dom in our minds. In Jesus' name we pray, Amen.

Abraham Lincoln's Gettysburg Address has been called America's "greatest gathering of words."[1] Lincoln's message was given over 130 years ago on the Civil War battlefield in Pennsylvania named Gettysburg. The burial of the Union dead was still underway on November 19, 1863, when Lincoln delivered his speech. We should not forget that it was a cemetery that the president had been invited to dedicate that day.

What makes the Gettysburg Address the greatest speech in American history is the way in which Lincoln gave firm definition to that famous proposition written by Thomas Jefferson in the American Constitution, that "Four score and seven years ago, our fathers brought forth upon this continent, a new nation, conceived in liberty, and dedicated to the proposition that all people are created equal."

The power of President Lincoln's speech is carried out in those five simple words — that all people are created equal. Now, we know, of course, that from the perspective of human judgment, men and women are certainly not created equal. We know that there are differences between us in personality, in intelligence, in natural talents, in bodily appearance and in physical strength and ability.

We also know that some people are born, as they say, with a "silver spoon in their mouth." These are the ones, of course,

59

who are born with the advantages of wealth and privilege and family connections which open doors and make life comfortable and pleasant and enjoyable.

And then of course there are those who are born literally with nothing at all, children who are so poor that they do not even receive proper nourishment, and therefore suffer from malnutrition and disease. Others suffer from physical abuse and neglect.

A recent study indicated that poverty among children spread rampantly throughout the 1980s from large urban centers to smaller United States cities. More than one-fourth of children living in cities are impoverished. Such widespread child poverty threatens our children's health, their ability to learn, and their opportunity to lead quality lives.

No, the hard, cold truth is that we are not created with equal circumstances. But the point of the phrase, "all people are created equal," says to us that this is indeed how God sees the men, women and children whom he has created. God's love is not withheld from any person, regardless of his or her circumstances. And we as Christian people are called to do likewise. We are called to be like our Father in heaven in the way in which we treat other human beings.

In our gospel lesson for the morning, Jesus tells a parable which reveals a truth of God that is very disturbing to the conventional, human way of seeing the world. Indeed, President Clinton would not have been elected had he tried to sell the economic policy described in this parable.

Jesus tells of a landowner who went out to hire workers for his vineyard. He agreed to pay them one denarius, which was a better-than-average wage for a day's work. In those days, such a verbal agreement for pay was considered to be legally binding. And so the men begin their work at dawn in what was usually a 12-hour workday, from dawn to sunset.

However, the landowner realized three hours later that more help was needed. And so he saw other persons standing around with nothing to do, and he offers them work. He did the same thing six and then nine hours later. Even at the

11th hour, with only one hour of work left in the day, the landowner offered work to those who wanted it.

Now the problem arose when the time came to pay up. The landowner directed his assistant to pay each of the workers the same wage — which was one denarius, again, a generous pay for one day's work.

This was quite a surprise, to say the least. The men who had worked all day, from sunrise to sunset, began to grumble. They felt it was unjust that the men who had worked just one hour would receive the same pay as those who had worked 12 long and hard hours. They felt that because of these circumstances, they should receive more money for doing that which they had agreed to do for one denarius.

But the landowner tells them to take what rightfully belonged to them and to go home. As the master of the vineyard, the man believed, quite rightly, that he was free to give what he wanted to the people he had hired, as long as he had fulfilled his basic agreement. He was free to be just as generous as he liked.

This of course bothered the workers. But the landowner asks, in effect, this difficult question of the disgruntled workers: "Am I not allowed to do what I choose with what belongs to me? Or are you envious because I am generous?" Jesus concludes, "So the last will be first, and the first will be last."

As Neal Fisher suggests, in the parable of the workers in the vineyard, the point is not the wage policy of the employer. Rather we have here a situation in which the sheer, immeasurable grace of God is at work in a surprising way.[2]

The parable is addressed to the Pharisees, men who had spent their entire lives carefully attending to even the smallest details of religious life. They had spent their lifetimes doing what they thought was "right" in the eyes of God. Because of the sacrifices they had made, they thought that they deserved to be richly rewarded. The Pharisees were offended by the idea that those who had not engaged in life-long serious study of God's Word and holy law could at a late hour walk into God's kingdom alongside those who labored for that reward all of their lives.

The point of Jesus' teaching is that it is not the industriousness of the laborer that counts. The message of the parable is the great goodness that God shows to all of the workers in his kingdom, regardless of when they come in to live and to work.[3]

All people are created equal. That, my friends, is the way that God thinks of us, no matter what our opinion is of this very unconventional way of thinking about and assessing human value. There are those who think they have earned what they have, rather than seeing their opportunities and accomplishments as gifts from God. There are those who may think that they have earned a special place in society or even in heaven because of what they have done as good persons.

But God does not measure you and me by worldly standards. He does not count how many hours we have worked. God does not look at how much stuff we have accumulated. The teaching here is clear. God sees us equally. God treats us equally. We deserve nothing on our own. Everything we have is a free gift from God.

The great English mystic Thomas Traherne in the 17th century advises us to enjoy the whole world, indeed the whole universe, and to be grateful for all of it. If we view God's world in this way, then we can see a beauty and experience a joy of which legal owners of property may never dream.[4]

We can indeed be owners of nothing, and yet be possessors of all things in God. We are created equal in our calling to recognize the loving power of God in every created thing. Because it is when we begin to seek out the love and power of God in the world in which we have been created equal to all other humans that we can thereby be truly surprised by God's grace and God's love.

Are not you and I surprised by God's grace each and every day we live? Are you not thrilled by the goodness and greatness of God? It doesn't matter who you are or what you have done, it does not matter where you live or how much money you have in the bank. God's love and grace is free, and it is there for all to experience.

Do we not need this word of hope in our world today? A psychologist once conducted a poll. He asked people: "What do you have to live for?"' He was surprised and shocked to learn that 94 percent were just enduring the present, while they waited for the future. They were all waiting for "something to happen."

Some of these people were waiting for the children to grow up and leave home. Some were just waiting for next year, hoping that things would be better. Others were waiting to take a trip which they had dreamed about for a long time. Some were waiting for retirement. Others were waiting to die.

As I read the New Testament, and especially these parables of Jesus, I think we get the very clear message that we should be living for today. We live in a new age which has been inaugurated by the life, death and resurrection of Jesus Christ. Each and every day we can be surprised by the beauty and wonder of the sheer grace of God.

George Bernanos, in a book titled *Diary of a Country Priest,* describes the ministry of a humble and unsuccessful country pastor. Most of the time the pastor is inept. The bored villagers he serves ignore him, his church all but deserts him. There is one wealthy parishioner who is particularly harsh on the poor minister. In part this is because of her personal bitterness toward God.

However, as this woman draws near death, the priest somehow manages to break through the barriers and helps this woman to surrender her life to God. With his help, she is able to believe in eternal life.

The pastor shares these words with the woman at the moment of death. "Be at peace," he tells her. And as the woman kneels to receive this peace of Christ, the pastor prays to God: "May she keep it forever; it will be I who gave it to her." He prayed, "Oh miracle — thus to be able to give what we ourselves do not possess, sweet miracle of empty hands. Hope which was shriveling in my heart flowered again in hers; the spirit of prayer which I thought lost in me for ever was given back to her by God and — who can tell — perhaps in my name!"[5]

My friends in Christ, have you ever experienced the "miracle of empty hands?" Have you ever felt inadequate and unsure of yourself as you have tried to help someone who was hurting, someone who was in deep emotional pain? It happens to pastors quite often. We utter stumbling words and prayers that we do not feel are fitting or adequate for the situation. We feel awkward and think that we are bothering a person who needs his rest. And yet that parishioner will later say to us that our prayers and visits were very comforting.[6]

When this happens, we should remember the miracle of empty hands. Because we never know how the Spirit of God will work in and through us, both pastors and lay persons. This is what it means to be surprised by grace.

Brothers and sisters in Christ, we do indeed have something great and wonderful to live for in this world in which God has placed us. It is so easy to get down and depressed about that which is happening to us and all around us.

But if we are able to lift our eyes to heaven, and open our hearts and minds to the unlimited love of God, we will experience the beauty and wonder of the world all around us. We can be "surprised by grace" in our homes, at work, and especially in this church where so many good things are happening every week. All that we need are eyes to see the good, voices to praise and thank the Lord, and hearts in which to feel the peace of Christ and the presence of God. God in Christ will always be there for you if you let him. Why not give him your all this day? Because this inaugurated is the way that God intends for us to live in the new age by the life and resurrection of our Lord Jesus.

My prayer for you this day is that you may be surprised by grace in all that you do. May you be blessed in your service of Christ now and always.

Benediction: Let us pray: Gracious and everliving Father, we have worshiped together and shared love with one another. We have experienced your grace among us in your house. As we go from this place, may we look for your love in encounters we have with others. Amen.

[1]William Mcfeely, "How We Were Created Equal," *New York Times Book Review,* June 7, 1992, p. 1.

[2]Fisher, *The Parables of Jesus,* p. 88.

[3]*Ibid.,* p. 87.

[4]H. Boone Porter, *The Living Church,* October 13, 1991, p.

[5]George Bernanos, *Diary of a Country Priest* (Toronto: Macmillan, 1937), p. 157.

[6]This insight is from an unknown source.